WASHINGTON, D.C.
THEN AND NOW

WASHINGTON, D.C.
THEN AND NOW

69 Sites Photographed in the Past and Present

Selection, Contemporary Photographs, and Text by
CHARLES SUDDARTH KELLY

Dover Publications, Inc., New York

This book is dedicated to all photographers whose views of the capital have come down to us. My grateful commendations to those who saved their pictures; my remonstrations to those who did not.

Published in Canada by General Publishing Company, Ltd., 30 Lesmill Road, Don Mills, Toronto, Ontario.
Published in the United Kingdom by Constable and Company, Ltd.

Washington, D.C., Then and Now: 69 Sites Photographed in the Past and Present is a new work, first published by Dover Publications, Inc., in 1984.

Manufactured in the United States of America
Dover Publications, Inc., 31 East 2nd Street, Mineola, N.Y. 11501

Library of Congress Cataloging in Publication Data
Kelly, Charles Suddarth.
    Washington, D.C., then and now.

    1. Washington (D.C.)—Description—Views. 2. Historic sites—Washington (D.C.)—Pictorial works. 3. Washington (D.C.)—History—Pictorial works. I. Title.
F195.K44 1984   917.53′00222   83-5313
ISBN 0-486-24586-1

INTRODUCTION

From the circling heights of the northern part of the District to the river banks on the south, as far as the eye can reach, are ponderous domes and majestic spires, countless turrets and roof-tops, emerald-tinted parks, massive monuments, and all the evidence of a prosperous city. This is the city of Washington as it appears today—a charming city of parks and palaces and the grand seat of government . . . of the United States of America.

Except that most of the turrets have disappeared, these words, written a century ago (by Joseph West Moore in *Picturesque Washington*, 1887), could well describe the Washington, D.C., of today.

Not that there have been no changes in the nation's capital since then. On the contrary. Despite the persistence of much of its character and many of its landmarks, the Washington of today differs vastly from the Washington of 1887, and yet more enormously from the Washington of 1846, the year of the first photograph in this book. These profound changes have consisted, in part, of the belated realization of plans for the Federal city that were conceived as far back as 1791. In part the changes stem from the planned and unplanned growth of the city as the seat of the Federal government. And, in part, the changes, like those of many American cities, have followed familiar patterns of commercial and residential expansion and decline, including many a curious happenstance of preservation or demolition.

The 150 photographs in this book document the growth of our nation's capital from the early days of photography through the present. The photographs are arranged in 69 sequences, each containing one or more archival views (specially selected by the present author) and one or more contemporary views. The latter were taken by the author from the same or nearly the same camera locations and angles as those of their archival counterparts. Each sequence consequently records the changes at a particular Washington location over a period of many years; a few sequences, comprising from three to six photographs each, show the changes at their locations in several stages over a century or more.

When in 1800 the Federal government officially moved to the city of Washington in the territory of Columbia on the Potomac ("River of the Swans" to the Indians), the new national capital consisted of a handful of partly completed government buildings and a few hundred residences surrounded by cornfields, tobacco patches, orchards, woods, springs, creeks, marshes,

and vestiges of Indian villages. What was to become Lafayette Square was then a cherry orchard covering most of an old Indian burial ground. Some seventy years afterward, despite extensive development, most of the streets yet remained unpaved. Moreover, development was haphazard, the original plans of the founding fathers having been virtually forgotten. From 1871, when widespread street paving and improvements were begun under Alexander Shepherd, through the early twentieth century, when the influence of the plans of the McMillan Commission began to be felt, through the implementation of the Federal Triangle project, the more recent plans of the Pennsylvania Avenue Development Corporation, and similar undertakings, the growth of the Federal city has proceeded by stages. Today, as can be seen clearly in the photographs in this book, central Washington, with its broad boulevards lined with magnificent classical structures and its numerous monuments, squares, and parks, in many respects conforms more closely to the capital city envisioned by the founders than did any intervening architectural metamorphosis.

The process of change is far from complete. In the course of preparing this book, I have had to rephotograph many sites more than once as current projects continue to alter the face of many sections of the city. Change has added another obstacle: that of gaining access to vantage points used by the photographers of early views. I have had to rely on the cooperation of many organizations (whose names are gratefully mentioned below) to accomplish what in some instances was much easier for the photographer of long ago. Arrangements were made to open the thick glass windows at the peak of the Washington Monument; open the long, winding stairways leading to, and platforms at the top of, the Capitol's dome; put a box step under the suspended ladder to the trapdoor of the turreted tower of the Smithsonian's main building; and gain access to many other rooftops and office windows. I have had to rely on similar cooperation to gain permission to place a tripod in the middle of the street and on the steps of government buildings and memorials. In a few instances, where for example a building has taken the place of a street, duplicating the exact point of view of an older photograph has not been possible, and a close approximation has been made.

The order of the photographs is, as far as practicable, that of a tour beginning at the Capitol and proceeding northwest toward Georgetown.

ACKNOWLEDGMENTS

While moving about Washington to search out old photographs and take new ones, I enjoyed the cooperation and encouragement of many organizations. They provided archival photographs, made necessary arrangements, opened the way to ordinarily inaccessible locations, granted permissions, and furnished guidance and helpful information. My thanks to the staffs and members of the following organizations: the Columbia Historical Society; the Washingtoniana Collection at the Martin Luther King Memorial Library (D.C.); the Peabody Collection at the Georgetown Public Library; the Junior League of Washington; Prints and Photographs Division, Library of Congress; the National Archives and Records Service; the District of Columbia Department of Highways and Traffic; the National Capital Regional Office, National Park Service, U.S. Department of the Interior; the Office of the Curator of the "Castle," the Smithsonian Institution; the Washington Gas Light Company; the Office of the Architect of the Capitol; the United States Capitol Historical Society; the Office of the Historian, Committee on the District of Columbia, U.S. Congress; the Commission of Fine Arts; the Pennsylvania Avenue Development Corporation.

The following individuals always gave generous attention to my inquiries, extended the courtesies of their offices, or opened the files of their own collections: Mr. James M. Goode, author, and Curator of the "Castle," the Smithsonian Institution; Mr. Perry G. Fisher, author, and Executive Director, Columbia Historical Society; Mr. William H. Leary, Managing Editor, *Picturescope* magazine; Dr. and Mrs. Douglas Woods Sprunt, on behalf of the Junior League of Washington; Mr. Volkmar Kurt Wentzel, author and photographer; Mr. Hugh Talman, master photographic printer; Dr. Klaus Hendriks, Chief, Photographic Preservation, Archives of Canada; Mr. Marc L. Davis, Prints and Photo Curator, the Washington Gas Light Company; Mr. Robert Lyle, Librarian of the Peabody Collection at the Georgetown Public Library; Mr. Emil Press, photographic historian; Mr. Fred Schwengel, President, the United States Capitol Historical Society; Mr. Nelson F. Rimensnyder, Historian, Committee on the District of Columbia, U.S. Congress; and my especially kind friend, Mr. Bryson Rash, author, historian, and senior television journalist, specializing in the history of the capital.

In particular I would like to acknowledge the patient, tireless, and never-failing assistance of Mr. Robert A. Truax, given first in his former capacity as Curator of Prints and Photographs at the Columbia Historical Society, afterward as an intrepid historical detective and unfaltering authority on the District of Columbia, as curator of his own archives and memorabilia, and as a respected consultant.

My editor at Dover, Alan Weissman, expertly turned my original essays and results of my research into concise captions. And my appreciation to Mr. Hayward Cirker, President of Dover Publications, whose patient and undiminished interest has made this book possible.

PHOTOGRAPH CREDITS

Archival photographs in this book are from public, institutional, corporate, and private collections. In many cases the same photographs may be found in two or more collections. Credit to a particular organization or individual, therefore, does not necessarily imply exclusive possession by that source. Such credit merely indicates the immediate source of photographs used by the author. All references below are to page numbers.

Columbia Historical Society: 12, 18, 22, 24, 30, 38, 40 (bottom), 42, 44, 60, 66, 76, 78, 80, 90, 96, 102, 108, 134, 144.
Commission of Fine Arts: 114.
Corcoran Gallery of Art: 70.
District of Columbia Department of Highways and Traffic: 86, 88, 128.

Library of Congress: 2, 26, 40 (top), 64, 74 (top), 98, 136, 138.
Martin Luther King (D.C. Public) Library, Washingtoniana Collection: 28, 34, 54, 58, 84, 100, 146.
National Archives: 4 (top & bottom), 8, 10, 20, 36, 46, 49, 50, 51, 56, 62, 68, 72, 74 (bottom), 82, 92, 94, 104, 106, 110, 112, 118, 120, 124, 126, 130, 132, 140.
Robert A. Truax: 6 (bottom), 14, 16, 48, 123, 142.
U.S. Department of Agriculture: 116.
Washington Gas Light Company: 122.

All current photographs are by Charles Suddarth Kelly.

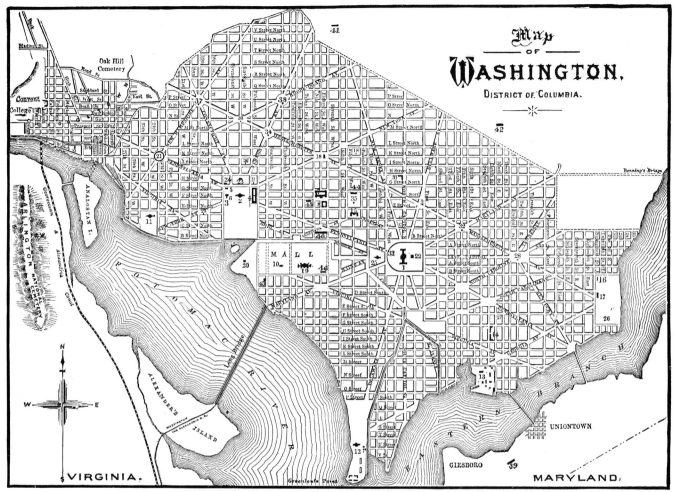

1. The Capitol. 2. The White House. 3. Department of State. 4. Treasury Department. 5. War Department. 6. Navy Department. 7. Patent Office. 8. Post-Office Department. 9. Department of Justice. 10. Department of Agriculture. 11. National Observatory. 12. United States Barracks. 13. Navy Yard. 14. Marine Barracks. 15. District Court House. 16. District Jail. 17. Washington Asylum. 18. Liberty Square. 19. Smithsonian Institution. 20. Washington Monument. 21. Washington Circle. 22. Statue of Washington. 23. Lafayette Square. 24. Corcoran Gallery of Art. 25. Botanical Garden. 26. Congressional Cemetery. 27. Naval Hospital. 28. Lincoln Square. 29. Rawlins Square. 30. Scott Square. 31. Government Printing-Office. 32. Greene Square. 33. Naval Monument. 34. Thomas Circle. 35. Judiciary Square. 36. McPherson Square. 37. Dupont Circle. 38. Iowa Circle. 39. Government Hospital for the Insane. 40. Center Market. 41. Howard University. 42. National Deaf Mute College. 43. Bureau of Printing and Engraving. 44. Pension Office. 45. Medical Museum. 46. National Museum.

Map of Washington, D.C., in 1887.
From Picturesque Washington: Pen and Pencil Sketches,
by Joseph West Moore
(Providence: Reid, 1887).

1

The United States Capitol, East Plaza (1846)

This view of the east side of the Capitol, from an 1846 daguerreotype by John Plumbe, Jr., is the oldest known photographic image of the Capitol and the only one of the Capitol in its second stage of completion. "Congress House," as it was called in the first of its three stages of construction, was begun in 1793 and, still uncompleted, was burned by the British in 1814. A reconstructed Capitol, based on the remains of the original, rose slowly. It was ready for occupancy in 1820, the interior was finished in 1824, and the center section and wooden dome completed in 1827. The design for the dome was by Charles Bulfinch, who also completed the rest of the building after the resignation of its original architect, Benjamin H. Latrobe. Today, all that remains of this dome is the interior rotunda.

The United States Capitol, East Plaza (1981)

The third and final stage of the construction of the Capitol, a massive enlargement, was largely the work of Thomas U. Walter. Begun in 1851, it too was completed gradually. The House of Representatives occupied the south wing in 1857, the Senate the north wing in 1859. The dome as we know it today was not completed until 1863. The two pedestals and street lanterns on either side of the street at the entrance to the plaza were installed in 1872 according to the landscaping plans of Frederick Law Olmsted, Jr. In 1958 the center pediment, portico, arcade, and steps were dismantled and extended forward, away from the building, by 33 feet. This work was done to align the center section with the left and right wings and to provide greater support for the dome. In both the 1846 and 1981 photos, structures can be seen that date back to the earliest days of the Capitol: on the Senate side (right), a small dome built in 1800, and on the House side (left), a small dome built in 1807.

(1860)

(1862)

(1981)

The United States Capitol, West Plaza (1860, 1862, 1981)

The 1860 photograph, taken between July and October of that year, shows work in progress on the Capitol in its final stage. The dome, the last major part to be completed, has risen to include the 34 columns of the colonnade and part of the section above it. In the foreground of this view is an overgrown, caved-in section of the abandoned Tiber Canal, a feature of L'Enfant's original plan for the city. It was dug in 1802 and abandoned as early as 1820, having become an eyesore and a stagnating health hazard. The small structure in the middle ground to the right is the greenhouse of the Congressional Botanic Garden, located at First Street, S.W. Designed by Thomas U. Walter, it was completed in 1859.

The 1862 view shows the dome nearer completion. Taken from a closer vantage point than the 1860 photograph, it also shows more clearly the tall fence of iron rods (stretching behind the greenhouse to the right), with nine entrance gates marked by sturdy pillars, that had been erected in 1830. The fence and gates were removed in 1882 (two of the pillars now stand on Constitu-

tion Avenue, between 15th and 17th Streets, N.W.). Behind this fence can be seen the thick forest that had grown there by the time of this photograph. The forest was replaced by a cultivated park landscaped by Olmsted, much of whose work, begun in 1872 and completed in 1890, remains today.

The contemporary view shows clearly the cross-braces added in the 1950s to reinforce the weakening columns on the west front. In the foreground are the Grant Memorial and the Reflecting Pool. The Memorial, consisting of a cavalry charge (far left), an artillery caisson (far right), and an equestrian statue of Grant (center), was dedicated in 1922 by Vice-President Calvin Coolidge and General John J. Pershing. The meticulously detailed bronze ensemble represents 22 years of work by the American sculptor Henry Merwin Shrady. The statue of Grant can be seen to line up with the statue of Freedom atop the Capitol dome. The Reflecting Pool, supported by the roof of a long highway tunnel, is a recent innovation, completed by 1976.

5

(1890)

(1914)

(1980)

Mall Vista, Looking East from the Washington Monument (1890, 1914, 1980)

The Capitol is seen prominently across the Mall in the 1890 view from the top of the Washington Monument. The Monument, begun on July 4, 1848, and completed on December 6, 1884, reached a height of 555 feet, enabling observations to be made from a height of 504 feet. The landscaping of the Mall, begun in 1851, followed the plans of architect Andrew Jackson Downing. After 1872, railroad tracks cut through the woods of the Mall and terminated at the famous Baltimore and Potomac Station. The long train shed attached to the station can be seen stretching across the Mall in the photograph. Just east of the station is a cluster of residences and fashionable boarding houses of the founding generation. Nearer the south side of the Mall and farther west (in the middle distance) can be seen the prominent towers of the Norman-style "Castle," the original building of the Smithsonian Institution (1855), designed by James Renwick, Jr. To its right, reaching to what is now Independence Avenue, is the Museum of Arts and Industries (1881). Above the latter is the Army Medical Museum (1887) and, to the west below the "Castle," the original building of the Department of Agriculture (1868), designed by Adolph Cluss in the "Renaissance" style, with its formal garden to the left and several acres of glass-and-iron-roofed greenhouses below it, stretching to the bottom of the photograph.

After 24 years, several prominent changes are noticeable in the 1914 view of the Mall and vicinity, many of them implementations of the 1901 plans of the McMillan Commission. The railroad tracks and station on the Mall are gone, having been removed upon the completion of the new Union Station north of the Capitol in 1907. The large, domed building that has arisen on the left is the National Museum of Natural History (1911), part of the Smithsonian. Flanking the Capitol in the distance are the Senate Office Building (left, 1909) and the House Office Building (right, 1908), both designed by Carrère and Hastings. And in the lower right-hand corner are the two large, separated wings of the new Department of Agriculture building (1908), occupying the site of the Department's old laboratories and greenhouses.

The Mall of 1980, very different from that of 66 years earlier, began to assume its look in the 1960s as the landscaping, with its broad, straight, rectilinear avenues, was brought into closer conformity with the old plans of Major L'Enfant. Some familiar structures remain while a new array of buildings has sprung up. At the lower left is the Smithsonian's National Museum of American History (1964). Next—to proceed clockwise around the Mall—can be seen the old Natural History Museum with its new wings, added in 1965, and past that is the great National Gallery of Art (1941) and its new Annex (1976). Opposite, on the other side of the Mall (actually on the Capitol grounds), is the Botanic Garden building, erected in 1931 when the old building was razed. The rectangular, quadripartite structure that comes next is the National Air and Space Museum. Opened in 1976, it has become the most popular museum in the world. The circular building next to it is the Joseph H. Hirshhorn Museum and Sculpture Garden (1974). On the rear side of the older Smithsonian buildings is the Freer Gallery of Art (1923). At the lower right is visible part of the center section (1931) of the new Department of Agriculture building.

Facing the Capitol, New Jersey Avenue and C Street, N.W. (ca. 1865)

Before Union Station was opened, the charming Italianate-style Baltimore & Ohio Railroad Station, completed in 1855, was an important point of entry and departure for visitors to the capital. President Lincoln arrived here in 1861 to be inaugurated, and it was from this station in 1865 that his body began its funeral procession north. Many other presidents, including Garfield, Roosevelt, and McKinley, made use of this depot. Behind the station stands a multiple residence (with its four chimneys) originally built by George Washington in 1798 and extensively rebuilt after the 1814 fire. It was a well-known hotel until its demolition in 1914. (In 1907 it was the Hotel Burton.)

Facing the Capitol, New Jersey Avenue and C Street, N.W. (1981)

The lovely arboreal growth of nearly a century later is typical of modern Washington. Unfortunately, so is the glut of motor vehicles crammed into parking spaces along New Jersey Avenue under the trees.

Near Independence Avenue and First Street, S.W. (ca. 1934)

Squalor in the shadow of grandeur, slum dwellings like these stood in the close vicinity of the Capitol from about 1860 to 1950. After the Civil War, shacks in the capital became the home of thousands of freed slaves. By 1890, more than 30,000 people, most of them former slaves and their descendents, lived in ramshackle alley dwellings in slum districts behind Washington's pantheons and parks. As late as 1937, some 9,000 houses were still lighted by oil lamps, 7,000 multifamily tenements were without inside running water, and 11,000 families had no inside toilets.

Near Independence Avenue and First Street, S.W. (1981)

More than half a million black Americans now reside in the District of Columbia (about five-sixths of its total population). Numerous urban-redevelopment projects have removed most of the old shacks. Those that stood on the site of this photograph have been replaced by the Rayburn House Office Building (behind the camera), opened in 1965 as the newest of three buildings for Representatives and their staffs. (The massive structure has necessitated a somewhat different camera angle in this photo.)

First Street and A Street (now Maryland Avenue), N.E. (1862)

Built in 1815 as the temporary house of assembly for the U.S. Congress after the British had burned the Capitol, this old "Brick Capitol" later became a fashionable boarding house and served other functions as well, until 1862, when it was made the principal Civil War prison in the capital. After the war, the "Old Capitol Prison" functioned as a fashionable residence and later as a school and offices, until it was demolished, by 1935, to make way for the new Supreme Court building. This photo has been attributed to Mathew Brady.

First Street and Maryland Avenue, N.E. (1980)

As recently as 1935, the U.S. Supreme Court held its sessions in the old Senate Chamber of the Capitol, until in that year the new Supreme Court building, seen in this photograph, was dedicated on the site of the Old Capitol Prison. The classic edifice of white marble was designed by Cass Gilbert. The flag is at half-mast in honor of Justice William O. Douglas.

Pennsylvania Avenue, N.W., from the Capitol (ca. 1905)

The 315-foot-high clock tower of the old Post Office building (1899) dominates this view of Pennsylvania Avenue. To the left, somewhat below it, is the Baltimore and Potomac Railroad station, which was soon to be torn down. Just to the left of the Post Office is the gleaming white marble roof of the new Corcoran Gallery of Art (1897; designed by Ernest Flagg); on the other side of the Post Office can be glimpsed part of the huge, 550-room, Second Empire-style State, War, and Navy Building, designed by Alfred B. Mullett and constructed at fantastic cost between 1871 and 1888 (it is still standing, renamed the Executive Office Building). The Greek Revival front visible at the end of Pennsylvania Avenue is that of the Treasury Building; to its right is the new Willard Hotel (1901). Lined with many other distinguished hotels, this stretch of Pennsylvania Avenue has been the major ceremonial avenue of the nation's capital for nearly two centuries. The Peace Monument can just barely be seen among the trees at the bottom of the photograph.

Pennsylvania Avenue, N.W., from the Capitol (1981)

The old Post Office, the Executive Office Building, and the Treasury remain, but the nearer part of this section of Pennsylvania Avenue has been entirely altered in 75 years. Many old buildings were razed for the Federal Triangle project, conceived in 1927 by Andrew Mellon but completed only gradually. The triangular plat of grass (opposite the Triangle itself) is surrounded by new buildings: the new Annex of the National Gallery (left), the Federal Trade Commission Building (at the apex of the Federal Triangle), the U.S. Courthouse (right of center), and the new Labor Department Building (right). The modern structure with the windowed stone canopy that seems to float above the buildings in the upper center belongs to the new J. Edgar Hoover F.B.I. Building, opened in 1975.

Pennsylvania Avenue East of 6th Street, N.W.,
Facing the Capitol (ca. 1905)

Pennsylvania Avenue as recently as this seemed hardly the Grand Concourse of the Republic, although it functioned as such. In the street in the distance are a street cleaner dressed in white, a gasoline-fueled automobile (the first of which was supposed to have chugged down Pennsylvania Avenue in 1896), and a streetcar, as well as various horse-drawn vehicles. The first building at the right carries the sign, scarcely visible here, of a wholesale whiskey dealer. The Patterson House hotel next door, occupying a Federal-style building, advertises rooms at 50¢ and 75¢, reflecting the prevailing rate of the neighborhood rather than the general economy of the times. The electrically powered delivery truck of Liebman Bros. Wholesale Grocers is backed up to the curb before a huge pile of boxes, evidently intended for a mid-nineteenth-century hotel building now apparently being used as a warehouse. The small white building beyond the George P. Killian paper-box company is on the southeast corner of 4½ (now 4th) Street. (See page 22.)

*Pennsylvania Avenue East of 6th Street, N.W.,
Facing the Capitol (1980)*

The statue representing man controlling trade (symbolized as a horse, right), a heroic allegory by Michael Lantz erected in 1942, stands in front of the Federal Trade Commission Building (not visible), at the apex of the Federal Triangle. Visible beyond the trees is the National Gallery, and to its left across 4th Street its new Annex—a great undecorated linear pile designed by I. M. Pei.

Pennsylvania Avenue and 3rd Street, N.W. (1917)

The New Capital Hotel, occupying the northeast corner of Pennsylvania Avenue and 3rd Street, had a long history. Originally the St. Charles Hotel, this Federal-style building was designed by Benjamin Latrobe and erected in 1820 with pilasters, capitals, and cornices that had survived the 1814 British invasion. Notable guests over the years included Hannibal Hamlin, Andrew Jackson, and Daniel Webster. Before the emancipation, the basement of the St. Charles functioned as one of at least three slave-market pens in Washington. In this 1917 photograph, the corner drugstore on the ground floor of the New Capital boasts a post-office station and offers the usual assortment of candy, soda, and cigars. The hotel was closed in 1924 and in 1926 the venerable little building was razed along with all of the blocks along Pennsylvania Avenue from 1st Street to 4½ Street.

Pennsylvania Avenue and 3rd Street, N.W. (1981)

Utterly different in character from the Federal-style New Capital Hotel is the Department of Labor Building that now occupies its site. The modern structure fills the entire block between 2nd and 3rd Streets, D Street, and Pennsylvania Avenue and provides work space for over 4,000 employees. A freeway tunnel runs underneath, its ventilation shafts rising through the roof of the building.

Northeast Corner of Pennsylvania Avenue
and 6th Street, N.W. (ca. 1940)

The National Hotel building shortly before its demolition in 1942. This distinguished establishment was created in 1826 when John Gadsby, proprietor of Gadsby's Tavern in Alexandria and the Franklin Hotel in Washington, converted a row of brick Federal-style town houses into a 200-room hotel. Andrew Jackson and Charles Dickens were among its most famous guests. After Gadsby died in 1844 the property passed into the hands of the Calvert family, who by 1857 had enlarged it to its final size. Henry Clay died there on July 1, 1852. Many times refurbished, the hotel was finally purchased for the District of Columbia government in 1929. In its heyday, one of its entrances was discreetly marked "Ladies."

*Northeast Corner of Pennsylvania Avenue
and 6th Street, N.W. (1981)*

On the site of the National Hotel now stands a building housing the District of Columbia Employment Security Agency, erected after World War II.

Pennsylvania Avenue and 4th Street, N.W. (1917)

This white brick Federal-style building on the southeast corner is the one pointed out in the distance in the view on page 16. Here it is The Hartford, a rooming house, advertising rooms at 25¢ and 50¢. On the ground floor is the Mee Nom Low Chinese & American Restaurant. Even today, the Chinese community of the capital lies within a few blocks of this location.

Pennsylvania Avenue and 4th Street, N.W. (1981)

After the old buildings on this site were razed in 1926, the ground remained a vacant grass plot until the East Building (Annex) of the National Gallery (opened in 1978) was erected there. The starkly linear structure was designed by I. M. Pei. It is connected to the West Building, the original building of the National Gallery, by a tunnel and an underground complex of rooms.

North Side of Pennsylvania Avenue
Between 6th and 7th Streets, N.W. (1911)

At the left in this 1911 photograph is the Central National Bank Building. No. 627 (1855), two buildings to the right, was from 1858 to 1881 the location of the Washington photographic studio and gallery of Mathew B. Brady, the great Civil War photographer. In those years he was also sought out by heads of state and other celebrities who came to have their photographic portraits taken. On the ground floor was Zadoc D. Gilman's Drug Store, still in operation at the time of this photograph. Its interior, a fine example of a nineteenth-century pharmacy, with elegant fixtures and decorations of the period, has been documented for all time in the Historic American Buildings Survey files in the Library of Congress. Three buildings to the right, and dominating the street, stands the Metropolitan Hotel, its facade essentially identical with that it assumed in 1850 when it was remodeled. Before that time it bore various shapes and names; it was then the Indian Queen Hotel, owned and operated by Jesse B. Brown, renowned among Washington hotel proprietors for his cordiality and hospitality. In 1850 Brown died, and his sons, responsible for the hotel's final remodeling, renamed it Brown's Marble Hotel. Finally, in 1865, under new ownership, it became the Metropolitan, the name it bore until its closing in 1933.

North Side of Pennsylvania Avenue
Between 6th and 7th Streets, N.W. (1981)

A very small part of the old Metropolitan Hotel remains in this recent view, the bulk of the building having been razed in 1935. Fittingly, the building that once housed Brady's studio is now occupied by a photography store on its ground floor (where Gilman's once was). That and the adjoining building, as well as the Central National Bank Building—here bearing the name "Apex"—are still standing after some seventy years, slated to be preserved and incorporated into a new group of structures that will bring new mercantile, office, recreational, and residential facilities to the block.

7th Street, Facing East Toward C Street, N.W. (1890)

At the extreme right is Pennsylvania Avenue. The Central National Bank Building, on the corner, is seen in this photograph from its 7th Street side. The building had assumed its present form in 1886, when architect Alfred B. Mullett expanded and remodeled an earlier structure on the site dating from 1859. Along C Street may be seen the rear of the well-known buildings fronting on Pennsylvania Avenue . The tall spire (left of center) is the Gothic needle of the Metropolitan Methodist Church, erected in 1854, completed in 1872, and demolished in 1936. The recently built white-marble building of the National Bank of Washington, in the "Richardson Roman-esque" style, stands between Louisiana (now Indiana) Avenue, at the left, and C Street.

7th Street, Facing East Toward C Street, N.W. (1981)

Both bank buildings in the 1890 photograph are still standing, though at the time of this photograph, the Central National Bank bore the name of Apex, a liquor store, the only occupant of the premises. In front of the National Bank of Washington stands the Grand Army of the Republic Memorial. The G.A.R., an organization of Union-army Civil War veterans, donated the cenotaph in 1909 to honor its founder, Dr. Benjamin F. Stephenson of Decatur, Illinois. Around the turn of the century the City Post Office building (extreme left) became a facility of the Central Union Mission, which it remains today.

Pennsylvania Avenue and 7th Street, Looking Southwest (1903)

Opened in 1801 as a group of sheds where farmers gathered to sell their produce (and known as "Marsh Market" because it was subject to flooding from a nearby creek), Center Market in 1873 occupied the building, designed by Adolph Cluss, that is shown prominently in this photograph. The mammoth facility stretched from 7th to 9th Streets and down to B Street (now Constitution Avenue). It sheltered a thousand stalls under one roof, offering to all classes of Washington residents, from senators' wives on down, a seemingly boundless supply of the finest fresh fruit, meats, poultry, fish, and dairy products. When this photo was taken in 1903, Center Market was in its prime, well maintained, electrified, and with full refrigeration facilities. At Washington's transportation hub, it drew shoppers from throughout the city. As the nation's largest market of its kind, it was a prime attraction for sightseers until its demolition in 1931.

Pennsylvania Avenue and 7th Street, Looking Southwest (1979)

The National Archives, housed in this imposing Greek Revival edifice designed by John Russell Pope and constructed under the provisions of the Federal Triangle Project, was opened in 1937 on the site of Center Market. Behind its walls are such treasures as the original Declaration of Independence, the Constitution, and the Bill of Rights, as well as hundreds of thousands of photographs, maps, motion-picture films, and other military and civilian records. The equestrian statue in the foreground (seen also in the 1903 view), created by Henry Ellicott in 1896, commemorates Major General Winfield Scott Hancock, a Civil War hero who narrowly lost the presidential election of 1881 to James Garfield.

*North Side of Pennsylvania Avenue,
Between 7th and 8th Streets, N.W. (1917)*

The four photographs in this sequence span the final 65 years in the life of a part of Market Space, the area across the Avenue from Center Market. The buildings in this 1917 view are second-generation structures, gradual replacements for the Federal-style buildings that had been erected in Market Space from 1791 to about 1850. In 1866 Sigmund Kann of Baltimore opened his dry-goods store in the Second Empire-style building on the 8th Street corner; by 1900, Kann's owned and occupied not only that and the center building but also the Saks & Company building on the 7th Street corner. As the sign proclaims, the complex was called "Kann's Busy Corner." The building with a cupola at the right is the Firemen's Insurance Company building.

North Side of Pennsylvania Avenue
Between 7th and 8th Streets, N.W. (1977)

This 1977 photograph shows Kann's in its final form, though it had been closed for two years. The aluminum front had been erected in 1959 to unify the buildings.

North Side of Pennsylvania Avenue,
Between 7th and 8th Streets, N.W. (1979)

Unfortunately the aluminum front also aggravated the effects of a mysterious fire on
February 2, 1979, that damaged the buildings beyond repair.

North Side of Pennsylvania Avenue,
Between 7th and 8th Street, N.W. (1981)

The block is part of a much larger area that has been slated for redevelopment. In the 1981 photograph, Market Space is once again open ground, if only temporarily. The old Firemen's Insurance Company building remains, but without its cupola.

Pennsylvania Avenue, Looking North Toward
8th Street, N.W. (ca. 1900)

This delightful photograph and that in the next sequence seem to be the work of one photographer. Pictured in this candid shot in Market Square (across from Market Space) are a sidewalk produce vendor and his customers on a sunny winter's day. On the other side of the streetcar is Kann's, though lacking the fourth story on the middle building that appears in the 1917 view (previous sequence). The buildings between 8th and 9th Streets are second-generation Pennsylvania Avenue commercial structures. Two buildings with distinctive curvilinear cornices, cartouches, and dentils stand out. The taller is 809 Market Space, erected in 1868. Its cast-iron Corinthian columns and neoclassic style were popular at the time.

Pennsylvania Avenue, Looking North Toward
8th Street, N.W. (1981)

Produce carts have not been seen at this location for over half a century, and what was once Kann's Busy Corner is now vacant. Only a few old buildings on Market Space remain, but they too are scheduled for demolition in the plans of the Pennsylvania Avenue Development Corporation. Visible behind them is the new F.B.I. Building.

7th Street, Looking Toward Indiana
(Then Louisiana) Avenue, N.W. (ca. 1900)

This view preserves for all time a moment in the street life of Market Square on a busy shopping day around the turn of the century. The Firemen's Insurance Company building, at 303 7th Street, N.W., in the center of the photograph, was erected in 1882.

7th Street, Looking Toward Indiana Avenue, N.W. (1981)

The Firemen's Insurance Company building remains, as do the three Federal-style buildings to its right. On the roof of L. Litwin's furniture building (at the right in the group) the faint lettering of the Uneeda Biscuit advertisement can still be detected. The new office building dates back about a decade before this photograph.

North Side of Pennsylvania Avenue,
Corner of 10th and D Streets, N.W. (1925)

The Franklin National Bank, in the building at the apex of the triangular block at the intersection, occupies the much enlarged Trader's National Bank building. To its left, with the Coca-Cola advertising, is the Ward's Dairy building (1884), which had become a furniture warehouse after about 1890. At the extreme left is a part of the old Washington Post building. The Romanesque building with the cupola, at 925 Pennsylvania Avenue (1895), is the home of Droop's Music Store, a Washington business since 1851. The entire area seen in this view was razed in 1963.

North Side of Pennsylvania Avenue at 10th Street, N.W. (1980)

The J. Edgar Hoover F.B.I. building, seen here, was completed in 1975 at a cost of $126,000,000, providing space for over 8,000 employees. Underground is a garage with 850 parking spaces. In the center is an open court. To accommodate this massive structure, an entire block of D Street (glimpsed in the 1925 view) had to be eliminated.

(1898)

(1925)

(1981)

North Side of Pennsylvania Avenue, Between 11th and 12th Streets, N.W. (1898, 1925, 1981)

The old Raleigh Hotel (at the left in the 1898 view) is located in the building opened as Shepherd's Centennial Building ca. 1876 and converted into a hotel in 1893. The taller building around the corner on 12th and E Streets, also belonging to the Raleigh, was built in 1898. In 1911 the tall Beaux-Arts-style building seen in the 1925 photograph replaced the converted Centennial Building. The new Raleigh stood only until 1964 when it and adjacent buildings were razed to make way for the Presidential Building (1981 photograph). The ornate facade of the Galt's Jewellers building remains the same in the 1925 photograph. In the 1981 photograph it has been entirely altered. In 1908 the old Evening Star Newspaper Buildings (1898 photograph) were replaced, except for a small portion remaining as an annex, by the taller structure seen in the 1925 photograph. By some preservationists' providence, this has avoided destruction (see 1981 photograph) while the even more interesting Raleigh Hotel, from the same period, has vanished. The *Evening Star* itself, founded in 1852, folded in 1981. Behind the *Star* building, the Hotel Harrington, in a structure completed in 1911 on 11th and E Streets, may be seen partly in the 1925 photograph and more fully in the 1981 view.

North Side of Pennsylvania Avenue,
Between 12th and 13th Streets, N.W. (1910)

The buildings seen here are an assortment of first- and second-generation structures. The tallest (except for the Raleigh Hotel across the street, at the extreme right) is the old office building, erected in the 1890s, of the Christian Heurich Brewing Company. Founded in 1873 by Christian Heurich, this Washington brewery brewed Senate Beer, Old Georgetown Ale, and other varieties until 1956.

North Side of Pennsylvania Avenue,
Between 12th and 13th Streets, N.W. (1984)

Two structures now fill the entire block, replacing all the older ones. The new Heurich Building, at the right, with the set-back angular facade, was completed in 1981 and represents a contemporary commercial utilization of space on the avenue. It was constructed by Skidmore, Owings & Merrill under the aegis of the Pennsylvania Avenue Development Corporation. Created by Congress in 1972, this agency strictly regulates all land use on the north side of Pennsylvania Avenue from the Capitol to 15th Street, N.W. (and may itself build, demolish, lease, and so forth). The older office building at the left, the McShain Building (1953), was built too early to have been affected by the regulations of the Corporation and so lacks the setback of the newer structure.

E Street Between 13th and 14th Streets, N.W.,
Looking North (1918)

This photograph was probably taken on a Sunday. On any other day the street would have been bustling with a mixture of visitors and residents that included shoppers, bureaucrats, and journalists. The Post Café, at the right, is so named because of the proximity of the Washington Post Building. Greason House, upstairs in the same first-generation building, was never among Washington's favored hostelries. The sign over "Shoomaker's Ladies' Millinery and Suits" indicates that the building probably dates from 1858. All the buildings on this block except the National Theatre remained much the same until they were razed in 1976. The National Theatre was opened in 1835, housed in the first of a succession of structures on this site. The building in this photograph, designed by Alfred B. Mullett, was opened in 1885. The sidewalk sign announces Otis Skinner in *Mister Antonio*. The National, fashionably attended for nearly a century and a half by government officials and diplomats, has become a national institution.

E Street Between 13th and 14th Streets, N.W.,
Looking North (1984)

The National Theatre, its facade having been extensively remodeled in 1922 and the entire building refurbished in 1983, is the only old building now remaining. To its right is 1301 Pennsylvania Avenue, The National League of Cities Building (1982), a new twelve-story project of the Pennsylvania Avenue Development Corporation. Its major tenant, the National League of Cities, is an organization that represents towns and cities across the country in their affairs with the Federal government. The brand-new Marriott Hotel (1984) dominates the rest of the block. At the extreme left, across 14th Street, part of the Willard Hotel is visible.

Pennsylvania Avenue Between 13th and 14th Streets, N.W.,
Looking Southeast (ca. 1903)

E Street is about to join Pennsylvania Avenue in the foreground of this photograph taken in 1903 or shortly thereafter. The Southern Railway Building (right of center), one of the two structures dominating this view—the other being the old Post Office (left)—is seen in its final form. In 1886, the Richmond and Danville Railway, a predecessor of the Southern, bought a newspaper building that had been erected on this site some fifteen years earlier. As the railroad grew by a series of mergers, the building grew as well, to three times its original size. The upper two floors and the tower, designed by William M. Poindexter, topped off the structure in 1903.

Pennsylvania Avenue Between 13th and 14th Streets, N.W.,
Looking Southeast (1981)

Except for the always-prominent old Post Office, nothing of 1903 remains in this 1981 photograph. The equestrian statue at the left, a monument to Brigadier General Count Casimir Pulaski, the Polish-born hero of the American Revolution, was erected in 1910, the work of sculptor Kasimir Chodzinski. The site of the Southern Railway Building is now a parking lot. Incorporating the site of a cluster of small commercial buildings, including a street-railway terminal, the New Post Office stands as it was constructed in the Thirties. The total Post Office as it had been planned was never completed. A mirror-image structure of the same hemicycle shape was to have been attached to the brick-faced wall of the western side of the present building, with the whole surrounding a central court. A similar extension planned for the eastern side can now never be constructed, as it would occupy the space of the old Post Office, which has been preserved as a landmark. The elevated median in the foreground is part of Western Plaza, a major feature in the Pennsylvania Avenue Development Corporation's design for the Avenue, intended to create the boulevard of grandeur that had been envisioned by the capital's founders. The inlaid patterns on the varicolored granite represent the founders' plan of the Avenue and environs. The gaily colored canopy at the right is intended as a place where strollers and government employees may relax.

Pennsylvania Avenue, N.W.,
Looking from the Treasury Toward the Capitol (ca. 1866)

This vista, shown in a sequence of photographs spanning 115 years, is the most photographed view of Pennsylvania Avenue. This ca. 1866 photograph is among the earliest extant of the view. The street was then still dominated by Federal-style row houses built around 1800 (the group of four at the right was called Treasury Row). The Willard and Solari's hotels, at the left, and the National Republican Newspaper building, with the mansard roof (right of center), are already seen.

ENNSYLVANIA AVENUE - 1885

Pennsylvania Avenue, N.W.,
Looking from the Treasury Toward the Capitol (1885)

The two hotels and the newspaper office are more prominent in this 1885 view, in which Shepherd's Centennial Building is now visible (left of center).

Pennsylvania Avenue, N.W.,
Looking from the Treasury Toward the Capitol (ca. 1905)

After the turn of the century, the towering Post Office, the Hotel Occidental, and the
G.A.R. building dominate. The Federal-style structures have all but disappeared.

Pennsylvania Avenue, N.W.,
Looking from the Treasury Toward the Capitol (1927)

In 1927, the new Raleigh Hotel dominates the center of the view.

Pennsylvania Avenue, N.W.,
Looking from the Treasury Toward the Capitol (1977)

The ill-fated Raleigh and most of the other buildings have been replaced after half a century (see also 1981 photograph) but the Hotel Occidental and the old Post Office staunchly remain. A District of Columbia office building (right) now occupies the site of the Federal houses. Treasury Row was razed in 1889 and its replacements demolished in the 1930s.

Pennsylvania Avenue, N.W.,
Looking from the Treasury Toward the Capitol (1981)

Changes in modes of transportation are also evident in this six-picture sequence. Horse-drawn streetcars running on metal rails were installed along the Avenue in 1862. Around 1890 they gave place to cars propelled by underground cables. After a fire at the cable power station in 1897, the cables were replaced by an underground electric third rail. Electric streetcars continued on the Avenue until 1962. The clutter of automobiles in the 1927 view has given way to that of buses and other modern vehicular traffic in 1977. In the most recent view, work of the Pennsylvania Avenue Development Corporation is seen in progress. Throughout the entire 115-year sequence, Treasury Plaza in the foreground and the Capitol, at the end of the Avenue, remain with few changes.

Looking Southwest from the Treasury (ca. 1896)

The building dominating this view is a photographic studio and laboratory serving the Treasury and probably other government departments. The studio is located under the extensive skylight at the front of the roof. In the yard behind the building are racks for hanging albumen print papers designed to be developed in the sunlight. The white tents scattered over the grounds south of the Treasury have been raised for a national convention of the Christian Endeavor Society. The Washington Monument, completed a little over a decade previously, rises in the background haze at the left. The familiar checkered stone flooring of the Treasury patio may be seen in the lower right-hand corner of the photograph.

Looking South from the Treasury (1981)

On the site of the old photographic studio is a memorial to General William Tecumseh Sherman, the famous Union Civil War general, and to the Army of the Tennessee. The equestrian statue, the work of Carl Rohl-Smith, stands 14 feet above the pedestal. At each corner of the stage stands a three-quarter life-size bronze soldier representing a separate force. After Rohl-Smith died in 1900, the ensemble was completed under the direction of Lauritz Hensen and Rohl-Smith's widow. It was finished in 1903. On the treasury patio stands a statue of Alexander Hamilton, the first Secretary of the Treasury. The statue, from an anonymous donor, was unveiled in 1923. It was the work of James Earle Fraser, a former assistant to the great Augustus Saint-Gaudens, and designer of the buffalo nickel. The benches and randomly placed pots of greenery are an invitation to the general public to use the plaza.

F Street at 15th Street, N.W., Looking East (ca. 1905)

This turn-of-the-century photograph shows vehicular traffic in transition, as an electrically powered delivery wagon (left of center) and streetcar (lower right) and a gasoline-powered car (in front of the wagon) mingle with horse-drawn carriages and wagons. At the left is Rhodes Tavern (about which more in the next sequence). Across the street at the right is the Corcoran Building (1875), in which is located a long-distance telephone center, the Delmar Cafe, and Lowdermilk's Book Store. The eleven-story building on the 14th Street Corner is a wing of the Willard Hotel (1901). The large street clock in front of it was a landmark from the moment it was built in 1902 until it was consigned to the war effort for its metal in 1942. On the near side of the Willard is the Union Trust and Storage Company building (1900). Across 14th Street, with flags flying, is the Ebbitt House hotel. Beyond that a partially obscured sign painted on the side of a building at 13th Street reads "Julius Garfinkel Bros., Cloaks, Suits, Neckwear, Imported Novelties." A bicyclist in typical attire is seen in the foreground with his wheels going in one direction and his eyes in another, as he is distracted by the woman in the white hat and flowing dress carrying a sheathed parasol.

F Street at 15th Street, N.W., Looking East (1981)

The Washington Hotel, at the right, replaced the Corcoran Building in 1917. Beyond it, to the left, is a parking garage, and between that and the Willard Hotel is an annex to the Willard, constructed in 1925 on the site of the Union Trust and Storage Company building. The Ebbitt House was replaced in 1926 by the National Press Club Building, providing offices and headquarters for journalists, press associations, newspapers, and magazines from around the world. Across from the Willard Hotel stands an expanded Garfinkel's. The Old Ebbitt Grill, at the left, took the great long bar, fixtures, and decorations from the old Ebbitt House when it closed in 1926. To the left of where the bicyclist passed in the older photograph, three-quarters of a century earlier, is a modern cyclist, less heavily attired but similarly distracted.

Northeast Corner of 15th and F Streets, N.W. (ca. 1925)

Rhodes Tavern (center), the oldest commercial building in downtown Washington, was so called after its first tenant, William Rhodes, who leased the recently completed Federal-style structure around 1800 from its owner, Bennett Fenwick, and operated a tavern and inn there. It would perhaps have been more felicitously named "Mrs. Suter's Boarding House," to recall the building's most notable moment in American history, in 1814. At that time, Mrs. Barbara Suter, widow of John Suter (owner of the famous Georgetown Tavern), had for seven years been operating her boardinghouse in what had been Rhodes Tavern, when the British invaded Washington. Having set many of the principal buildings ablaze, Admiral Cockburn and General Ross and their staffs marched up Pennsylvania Avenue, discovered Mrs. Suter's establishment on a side street, and arranged for meals and lodging for themselves and their officers. She could hardly refuse under the circumstances. Before returning late that night, they wreaked havoc in the capital, but to Mrs. Suter they were polite to the last. Beginning that same year, the building was occupied by a succession of tenants, including banks and several merchants. When the National Press Club was organized in 1913, for their first year they occupied the top floor of the old tavern building. In this photograph can also be seen the new building of the National Metropolitan Bank (1907; left), the first occupant of Rhodes Tavern after Mrs. Suter. At the right is the new home of Garfinkel's, still under construction.

Northeast Corner of 15th and F Streets, N.W. (1983)

Only the corner building of Rhodes Tavern now remains, and, at this writing, even its fate is in the balance. At present unoccupied, it is scheduled to be bulldozed along with adjacent structures to make way for an extension of an adjoining office building.

F Street at 14th Street, N.W., Looking East (ca. 1915)

Formerly a select residential area, F Street had by this time replaced Pennsylvania Avenue as the center for the city's finer stores. Between 10th and 14th Streets it had become known as the Bon Ton Shopping District and was also a center for photographic studios and moving-picture theaters. The building with the mansard roof at the right is the Ebbitt House hotel, erected in 1872 by Caleb Willard, brother of the owners of the Willard Hotel. Among the most fashionable hostelries of its day, the Ebbitt was a favorite of journalists, and their offices on the ground and basement floors had become known as "Newspaper Row." Before his inauguration in 1897, William McKinley lived at the Ebbitt. The awnings, the lady's parasol, and the straw hat on the man in front of the electric streetcar are signs of summer, though strictures of the time prevented the more matronly ladies from dressing accordingly.

F Street at 14th Street, N.W., Looking East (1980)

The Ebbitt House was razed in 1926 and the huge National Press Club Building erected on the site of old "Newspaper Row." Until 1963, the building also housed the Fox (after 1936, the Capital), an enormous movie theater seating 1,700. A median strip with trees now occupies the center of F Street where the streetcar tracks once ran. Many of the buildings on the north side of the street (left) remain.

15th Street at G Street, N.W., Looking South (ca. 1863)

This fine mid-nineteenth-century view shows the east facade of the partially finished Treasury Building, with its imposing Ionic colonnade. This was the third building to house the Treasury Department, the first having been destroyed by the British in 1814 and the second having burned in another fire in 1833. The present structure was authorized in 1836, and in 1839 the Treasury Department moved into the unfinished building. The Greek Revival edifice was designed by Robert Mills (except the wings, which were designed by others following Mills's style); when completed in 1869, it included 488 rooms and had cost over $6,000,000. Next door in this photograph is the charming old State Department Building, which stood until it had to be razed to make way for the north wing of the Treasury Building. From 1869 until its new quarters were completed a few years later, the State Department was housed in the Treasury Building. The unfinished Washington Monument is visible at the left in the photograph.

15th Street at G Street, N.W., Looking South (1980)

The north wing of the Treasury Building, finished in 1869—the last part of the Treasury to be completed—stands out prominently in this recent photograph. The Washington Monument (completed in 1884) rises in the distance. On 15th Street, modern automobiles ride where there were once horsecar tracks.

Northeast Corner of New York Avenue
and 15th Street, N.W. (ca. 1883)

The building on the corner, the Plant Building (after 1856), was the home of the National Safe Deposit Company and the National Savings Bank. The photograph captures the feel of a busy day as pedestrians, a horsecar, and a hansom cab wend their respective ways and the horse-drawn wagons of George Bogus, a firewood dealer, clatter around the corner. The steeple at the far right belonged to the New York Avenue Presbyterian Church, famous as the church attended by several U.S. presidents. Many of the buildings in this view were used by government agencies because of the proximity of the Treasury (behind the camera) and the White House (only a block away). All presidential inaugural parades proceed, from right to left, around this corner.

Northeast Corner of New York Avenue and 15th Street, N.W. (1983)

The National Safe Deposit Company and the National Savings Bank merged to become the National Savings and Trust Bank. Their old headquarters was razed in 1888 and replaced by the building—twice enlarged, once in 1916 and again in 1925—seen on the corner in this photograph. The old and new facades were so carefully matched in style and in the color of their brick and stone that the additions are hardly discernible. The Widner Building, partly blocking the view of the church steeple, was constructed when the church was rebuilt in 1950.

*Pennsylvania Avenue, Looking East
to New York Avenue at 15th Street, N.W. (1922)*

This view from just north of the Treasury (see the fence columns, lower right) encompasses buildings from several different periods. At the left is the Riggs National Bank building, erected in 1898 for the firm founded in 1840 by W. W. Corcoran and George W. Riggs, Jr. The office building at the right was also built in the 1890s. The two shorter buildings to its left date from the 1850s. One of these, the corner building, was the George Washington Hotel and also had a ticket office for the Southern Railway. The relatively tall office buildings down New York Avenue were new at the time of this photograph (the taller is the well-known Bond Building), as was the Masonic Temple, the farthest building visible on the avenue.

*Pennsylvania Avenue, Looking East
to New York Avenue at 15th Street, N.W. (1982)*

The Washington Building has replaced the George Washington Hotel and other buildings on 15th Street. For some time, the S & W Cafeteria in the Washington Building was famous for its Southern-style food, while the Madrillon Restaurant in the Bond Building (its facade undergoing alteration at the time of this photograph) next door was known for its excellent French cuisine. In this view—as in the earlier one— the cupola of the National Savings and Trust Bank rises over the right side of the roof of the Riggs Bank. The Masonic Temple is now a theater showing X-rated movies.

The White House, 1600 Pennsylvania Avenue, N.W. (1861)

This photograph, attributed to Mathew Brady, shows the President's House, or, as it more frequently came to be called, the White House as it appeared during President Lincoln's term of office. This building is actually a reconstructed White House, the original having been burned by the British in 1814. The restored building was first occupied by President Monroe in 1817. The north entrance portico and columns, also in this view, were added in 1829. The statue in the front yard is of Thomas Jefferson. Created in 1834 by French sculptor Pierre-Jean David (David d'Angers), it was presented to the government by Naval Lieutenant Uriah P. Levy and placed in the Capitol Rotunda. When President Polk in 1835 had it placed in front of the White House, it became the first bronze statue to be erected out-of-doors in the city.

The White House, 1600 Pennsylvania Avenue, N.W. (1980)

Although the front of the White House looks much as it did in President Lincoln's day, nothing of the original building except its walls remains. Extensive structural changes were made under President Theodore Roosevelt in 1902, and the most extensive of all under President Truman, from 1948 to 1952. The statue of Jefferson on the lawn was returned to the Capitol in 1874.

Northeast Corner, 17th Street and Pennsylvania Avenue, N.W. (1874)

The old Corcoran Art Gallery building stands in this view as it looked around the time of its official opening in 1874. James Renwick, its designer, was also responsible for the original Smithsonian "Castle," St. Patrick's Cathedral in New York, and other notable structures. The original Corcoran was built to house the personal art collection of William Wilson Corcoran, the great financier and philanthropist. The building was finished in 1859, but it was soon commandeered as a Civil War storage depot. After the war, Corcoran restored the building and opened it to the public in 1874, with its salons lavishly furnished in high Victorian style and their walls covered from floor to ceiling with paintings, all from Corcoran's personal collection. Ten of the eleven original statues in niches on the west and south sides of the building can be seen in this photograph. The seven-foot-high figures, by the American sculptor Moses Ezekiel, represented Phidias, Michelangelo, Dürer, Raphael, Titian, Leonardo, Rubens, Rembrandt, Murillo, Canova, and the American artist Thomas Crawford.

Northeast Corner, 17th Street and Pennsylvania Avenue, N.W. (1981)

At the time of this photograph the old Corcoran building was being restored, although most of Ezekiel's statuary is gone. The building ceased to house the Corcoran collection in 1897, when the new museum three blocks south was opened. From then until 1960 it served as the U.S. Court of Claims. At first scheduled for demolition, it was saved by the personal appeal to President Johnson of S. Dillon Ripley, Secretary of the Smithsonian. It now houses the Smithsonian's Renwick Gallery and bears the distinction of being the oldest art-gallery building in the capital and one of the first buildings in the United States erected exclusively for the purpose of housing an art gallery. In the background at the left in the photograph may be seen the modern office buildings along Connecticut Avenue and K Street.

17th Street and New York Avenue, N.W., Looking West (ca. 1861)

Thirteen teams of horses and oxen led by a black crew (their chief wears a top hat and black frock coat) are hauling a solid column to the nearby Treasury Building, under construction from 1836 to 1869. The columns, along with stone slabs and other construction elements, were stored in this yard until needed. The three-story dark house obscured by trees (left) is the Octagon House (1798–1800; designed by William Thornton for John Tayloe), one of Washington's most distinguished Federal-style residences. It was used as a temporary executive office by President Madison when the British burned the White House in 1814.

17th Street and New York Avenue, N.W., Looking West (1981)

The Octagon House is still standing, having been secured against destruction in 1902 by the American Institute of Architects, whose recently built headquarters may be seen in part to the right of the historic residence. Behind the Octagon House is the General Services Administration Building (1916). New office buildings occupy the site of the old Pilliard Room & Coffee House. 1709 New York Avenue (1974; center) is a general office building, and the building at the right is the headquarters of the Federal Deposit Insurance Corporation (1962). The fence at the right borders the grounds of the Executive Office Building.

(1865)

(ca. 1948)

(1981)

Northwest Corner, 19th Street and Pennsylvania Avenue, N.W.
(1865, ca. 1948, 1981)

The handsome row of Federal town houses (ca. 1795) in the 1865 view—known as the Seven Buildings—was most famous as including the home of President and Mrs. Madison (the corner building) from October 1815 to March 1817 while the White House was being restored after the British invasion. The corner building became known as the House of a Thousand Candles after the night of Dolly Madison's festive reception for General Andrew Jackson. The building was also the home of Martin Van Buren before and, briefly, after he was inaugurated as eighth U.S. president. The Seven Buildings also provided offices for various government departments over the years. This Mathew Brady photograph was dated by the photographer April 1865, but it remains a matter of conjecture what the people are gathered for. At this time the Seven Buildings were the headquarters of Civil War Major General M. D. Hardin.

After the Civil War, the Seven Buildings had a mixed occupancy of street-floor stores and upper-floor offices and flats. The second building from the right had a story added sometime after 1865. At least six of the buildings remained until 1898, when the sixth (counting from the right in the ca. 1948 photograph) was replaced by the bay-windowed four-story building seen at the extreme left. The Peoples Drug Store in the corner building was an early member of what has since become a large chain.

A Peoples Drug Store remains on the corner but it is now housed in a modern office building erected in 1959, when the old House of a Thousand Candles and two of its neighbors among the Seven Buildings were demolished. The fourth and fifth of the original Seven remain, however, as does the four-story building of 1898.

North Side of H Street, East of Connecticut Avenue, N.W. (1917)

The Corcoran house, dominating this view, is substantially the work of James Renwick, who in 1849 enlarged a structure that had been erected about 1818 and was once the home of Daniel Webster. Renwick was commissioned by William Wilson Corcoran, who occupied the house until his death in 1888. The white Greek Revival residence next door was originally one of three; the other two were demolished to make way for the Romanesque Revival houses designed by Henry Hobson Richardson in 1885 for John Hay, the statesman (who lived in the house at the extreme right), and Henry Adams, the author and historian.

North Side of H Street, East of Connecticut Avenue, N.W. (1980)

The imposing edifice occupying the site of the Corcoran house (razed in 1919) is the Chamber of Commerce building. Designed by Cass Gilbert, architect of the Woolworth Building in New York City, this classical structure, with its rows of semidetached, fluted Corinthian columns, was dedicated in May 1925. Next door is the Hay-Adams Hotel, named by entrepreneur Harry Wardman after the houses it replaced in 1927.

Jackson Place, Opposite Lafayette Square, N.W. (1902)

The wagons, moving men, and policeman standing guard make it extremely probable that this photograph of Marcy House, 736 (originally 22) Jackson Place, was taken on June 20, 1902, the day that President Roosevelt and his family moved their personal effects there to allow the White House to be renovated. Marcy House, having itself been somewhat remodeled in 1890, was originally built ca. 1840–45 for William L. Marcy, Secretary of War under President Polk. Next door to Marcy House is Murtagh House (1850), built by the man who was the founder and editor of the *National Republican Newspaper* and an early supporter of the presidential candidacy of Abraham Lincoln.

Jackson Place, Opposite Lafayette Square, N.W. (1981)

Although recommended for demolition by the McMillan Commission, after two world wars and other delaying circumstances the houses on Jackson Place remained standing. Finally, though they had been slated for replacement by a new Federal-government office building, in 1960 President Kennedy caused the plans to be revised to include preservation and restoration of the old Jackson Place residences. Under the direction of architect John Carl Warnecke, formerly anachronistic modern structures, such as the one to the right of Marcy House in this photograph, were remodeled to conform to the nineteenth-century style of the street. The Federal office building was built, but on 17th Street, behind the Jackson Place town houses, as can be seen here. The house with the mansard roof at the extreme left in this view (not visible in the 1902 photograph) is Parker House (1861), originally the home of Peter Parker, a pioneer nineteenth-century missionary to China. The building was once the temporary quarters of the Bureau of Pan American Republics, predecessor of the Pan American Union and the Organization of American States.

15th and I ("Eye") Streets, N.W., Looking West (ca. 1925)

The building imperfectly seen at the left is the McLean house, one of Washington's largest and most opulent private residences of the time. Built for John R. McLean, the mansion was a substantial enlargement of an already much remodeled house on the site. This latest expansion was the work of John Russell Pope (who later designed the National Gallery). The massive office building in the background is the headquarters of the U.S. Veterans' Administration (1918), built on the site of the famous Arlington Hotel. The drivers of the horse-drawn carriages (center) are licensed tour guides who from this location would drive sightseers around Lafayette Square, the White House, the Washington Monument, and other parts of the city. To the right of the two women pedestrians is McPherson Square.

15th and I ("Eye") Streets, N.W., Looking West (1981)

In 1939 the McLean mansion was demolished. The Lafayette office building, seen here, was erected on the site in the same year. The Veterans' Administration building remains. The elegantly attired tour guides have been replaced, at least on this occasion, by a cluster of helmeted police officers with a row of motorcycles, required by some event at the nearby White House.

McPherson Square, N.W., Looking North (1910)

One of the capital's many Civil War monuments, the equestrian statue of General James Birdseye McPherson dominates the middle of McPherson Square in this photograph of 1910. General McPherson, commander of the Army of the Tennessee, distinguished himself in front-line combat and died on July 22, 1864, during Sherman's march through Atlanta. The 14-foot-high statue, designed by sculptor Louis T. Rebisso and made of the metal of captured cannons, stands on a pedestal presented by Congress. It was dedicated on October 18, 1876, at which time the surrounding square—already set aside as park land in the L'Enfant Plan—had its name changed from Scott Square to McPherson Square. The exuberant foliage obscures the view of buildings, like the Burlington Hotel, across K Street and on Vermont Avenue.

McPherson Square, N.W., Looking North (1980)

General McPherson continues to ride his bronze horse in the middle of his square. Many of the trees are gone, however, and the modern office buildings that line K Street and Vermont Avenue somewhat overshadow the statue. These buildings are all of about the same relatively limited height, the maximum height of office buildings in Washington being strictly limited by law.

I ("Eye") Street, 17th Street, and Connecticut Avenue, N.W.,
Looking Southeast (ca. 1900)

This turreted Romanesque Revival building was built for the Army & Navy Club in 1891. The club, whose membership had grown from fewer than a hundred to 650 in its first six years (it was founded in 1885), was badly in need of new quarters at the time. The neighborhood was one of clubs, and nearby were the Metropolitan, the Racquet, the Cosmos, the University, the City, and the Women's City clubs. The Corcoran house can be seen in the background in this view, and in the foreground is a bit of Farragut Square, from which the photograph was taken.

I ("Eye") Street, 17th Street, and Connecticut Avenue, N.W.,
Looking Southeast (1981)

The Army & Navy Club, along with adjoining buildings, was razed in 1962 to make way for the Chanin Building (center), one of many maximum-height office buildings going up in the Connecticut Avenue–K Street area at that time (more may be seen at the right). The new Army & Navy Club (extreme left) was built across the street in 1912. The Chanin's principal tenant is the international law firm of Hogan and Hartson. Part of the Chamber of Commerce building is visible behind the Chanin Building.

Connecticut Avenue at K Street, N.W., Looking Northwest (1895)

Connecticut Avenue, extending northwest from Lafayette Square to Dupont Circle and beyond, was in the late nineteenth century a fashionable residential street. The mansion at the right was built and occupied in 1872 by Alexander Shepherd, the controversial city administrator under Grant, responsible for grading and paving Washington's streets, laying sewers, planting trees, and making numerous other municipal improvements.

Connecticut Avenue at K Street, N.W., Looking Northwest (1980)

Before the Shepherd mansion was razed in the 1960s, it had served widely diverse functions, from that of the Chinese legation to that of the Troika nightclub. Lining both sides of Connecticut Avenue are the modern office facilities that began to appear in the neighborhood after World War II and continue to proliferate rapidly. The character of this area in the 1940s may be seen in the first photograph of the next sequence.

K Street at Connecticut Avenue, N.W., Looking West (1948)

Typical of this part of Washington in the 1940s, the buildings on K Street display a
fascinating architectural irregularity. Late-nineteenth-century town houses like those
seen here were gradually converted to commercial use after World War II, their fine
interiors being apportioned as office space. Mrs. Frances Hodgson Burnett, the famous
Anglo-American author, wrote *Little Lord Fauntleroy* (1886) while residing in a town
house on this street.

K Street at Connecticut Avenue, N.W., Looking West (1980)

For whatever reason, the pedestrians in this photograph seem more in a hurry than those in the 1948 view. The charming old town houses lining K Street were demolished in the 1960s and their sites gradually occupied by the maximum-height office buildings seen here.

HERALD SQUARE, WASHINGTON, D.C.

H and 13th Streets and New York Avenue, N.W., Looking West (1931)

The New York Avenue Presbyterian Church, erected in 1859, here displays a new steeple added in 1929 to replace one that had toppled in 1896. This intersection was unofficially known as Herald Square, after the four-story 1920s building at the right, housing *The Washington Herald* and *The Washington Times*. To the left of the newspaper building stands the old George Washington Hospital.

H and 13th Streets and New York Avenue, N.W., Looking West (1981)

The New York Avenue Presbyterian Church in this view is a new building, constructed in 1950 on the site of the old church. The office building behind it was erected at the same time. Further to the left is a vacant lot where for many years stood the Translux Theater Building (1936), containing the offices of station WMAL and the Washington studios of the National Broadcasting Company. The *Times* and the *Herald* were bought by *The Washington Post* and closed in 1949, but their building, with two additional stories, still stands. Next door, on the site of George Washington Hospital, a modern office building now stands. The office building in the center of this view, now bearing the single word "landmark," is visible in the 1931 view as the Continental Trust Company Building.

10th Street, Between E and F Streets, N.W.,
Looking Southeast (ca. 1861)

Ford's Theatre, made forever memorable by the assassination of President Lincoln on April 14, 1865, had been a theater for only about three and a half years before that tragic event, and for one or another reason (including a fire that substantially destroyed the original building) had been closed even during much of that time. From 1834 through 1859 the First Baptist Church occupied the original building and in 1861 the vacant structure was acquired by John T. Ford for use as a theater. The photograph dates from about the time of Ford's purchase. Ford's Theatre was closed after the assassination. The building was purchased by the government and in 1866 opened as an office building for the War Department. It continued as a government office and warehouse building for nearly a century. During the structure's brief period as Ford's Theatre, the house standing to its right was the residence of Harry C. Ford, who managed the theater for his father. The three-story building also housed the Star Saloon on the ground floor. At the time of this photograph, 10th Street, like most Washington streets before the 1870s, was still unpaved.

10th Street, Between E and F Streets, N.W.,
Looking Southeast (1980)

Ford's Theatre, since 1933 under the jurisdiction of the National Park Service, was approved in 1964 for restoration and in 1968 was reopened as a theater and museum. The restoration of the interior, of which no original furnishings remained, had to be undertaken with the aid of photographs that had been made by Mathew Brady. The little building to the left of the theater now provides access to the lobby and serves as a ticket office. The large building at the extreme left in this photograph, constructed in the 1960s, houses a garage and a women's apparel store. Next door to the old Star Saloon is the former headquarters of the Potomac Electric Power Company. Visible on the next block is the giant, ultramodern F.B.I. building.

Thomas Circle, Looking North (1925)

Only a few of the fifteen circles envisioned by Major L'Enfant ever materialized. Thomas Circle, centering on a statue of Major General George Thomas (1879), is one of these. At the time of this photograph, Thomas Circle, at the junction of Massachusetts and Virginia Avenues and 14th and M Streets, was a carefully landscaped circular park in the heart of a quiet residential neighborhood. The streetcar tracks bending around the circle were about a quarter-century old, but the electric street lamps standing around its circumference had recently, in 1923, replaced gas lamps. The residence at the right is the Wylie house (1843), once the home of Andrew Wylie, the distinguished Federal judge under Lincoln. In front of the Lutheran Memorial Church (1870) on the north side of the circle is a statue of Martin Luther (1884). The steeple farther to the right belongs to the Vermont Avenue Christian Church.

Thomas Circle, Looking North (1981)

No longer surrounded by a quiet residential enclave, Thomas Circle has been shrunk to accommodate the heavier flow of traffic around it. The streetcar tracks and ornamental lamps were removed in the 1950s. The two churches have remained and another, the National City Christian Church (left), was erected in 1930. The Wylie house was demolished in 1947, and now the International Inn, a modern hotel with a domed swimming pool, stands in its place.

Connecticut Avenue and California Street, N.W. (1909)

This intersection, on a hill northwest of downtown and somewhat removed from it, commands a broad view of central Washington. An equestrian statue (1907) of Civil War Major General George B. McClellan stands at the right. The Wyoming House was one of the most luxurious of Washington's apartment houses at the time of this photograph. Its spacious interior suites were finished with marble and fine carved woods.

Connecticut Avenue and California Street, N.W. (1981)

The Washington Hilton Hotel (right) now dominates this intersection, which, though congested with motor vehicles, has retained some of its genteel character. The awnings of Wyoming House are gone, rendered obsolete, presumably, by modern air conditioning. Some of the view long treasured by residents of the old luxury building has been usurped by guests of the modern hotel across the street.

Florida Avenue, Looking North along 16th Street, N.W. (1888)

The imposing mansion on the hill at the left, aptly named "Henderson's Castle," was built in 1888 for Senator John Brooks Henderson, drafter of the Thirteenth Amendment to the Constitution (abolishing slavery), and for his wife, Mary Newton Foote Henderson, a grande dame of Washington society. On Meridian Hill at the right stands the first building of Columbian College, erected in 1821 (Columbian moved away in 1870 and became George Washington University). Meridian Hill was originally Peter's Hill, named after Robert Peter, Mayor of Georgetown, who had assembled patents for the land in 1760. Near the end of the nineteenth century, Meridian Hill was unsuccessfully proposed as the site of the Lincoln Memorial and, alternatively, of a new White House.

Florida Avenue, Looking North along 16th Street, N.W. (1980)

Mrs. Henderson occupied Henderson's Castle until her death in 1931. The mansion was razed in 1949, although the stone retaining wall and crenellated entrance gates have survived. The old estate is now occupied by Beekman Place, a condominium development. From 1917 to 1936, twelve acres of Meridian Hill were turned into a magnificently landscaped public park, now maintained by the National Park Service. Meridian Hill Park is unfortunately plagued by crime, but community efforts are being made to reclaim it as as a safe recreation area. Sixteenth Street has become a major north-south artery.

7th and D Streets, N.W., Looking North (ca. 1895)

Seen here before the turn of the century, bustling 7th Street just north of Pennsylvania Avenue was at the shopping hub of the city, though it was less fashionable than F Street (which crosses 7th where the building with the mansard roof stands, center). The space, at the left, on the corner of F Street marks the grounds of the Patent Office (1836–69; designed by Robert Mills), and nearer still is the old city Post Office (1839–69; also designed by Robert Mills). Soon after the time of this photograph, the cable cars were electrified and the unsightly telephone poles removed as electric cables were laid underground.

7th and D Streets, N.W., Looking North (1980)

Seventh Street remained an important shopping district well into the twentieth century but went into serious decline after the riots of 1968. Some old buildings remain, some were radically altered or replaced after the turn of the century. The Post Office building (center) survives as the building of the Tariff Commission. The building with the mansard roof (top right), not clearly visible in the earlier photograph, is Odd Fellows Hall, built in 1846 and extensively rebuilt and remodeled over the years.

7th Street Between E and F Streets, N.W., Looking Northeast (1911)

From the mid-nineteenth century and for many years into the twentieth, 7th Street north of Pennsylvania Avenue, including this stretch, was one of the city's prime commercial areas. The Hechts Greater Stores building (center) is the first of what has since become a large metropolitan chain. The Second National Bank (right) occupies a notable cast-iron building.

7th Street Between E and F Streets, N.W., Looking Northeast (1980)

The Hecht Company remains on this site, one of a dwindling number of commercial establishments in this part of the capital. Although the original Hecht building is still standing (center) the greater part of the store occupies the newer building on the corner of F Street, built in 1949. The cast-iron building at the right, scarcely altered in seventy years, still houses a bank.

7th Street, Looking North from F Street, N.W. (ca. 1889)

A crew of track workers—and a crowd of well-dressed onlookers—pause for the photographer. The crew was laying a cable trough between the streetcar rails, part of Washington's new system of cable-drawn streetcars. Within a decade, the cables would give place to underground electric third rails. The U.S. Patent Office stands on the left. Numerous patent agents occupied offices in the buildings at the right.

7th Street, Looking North from F Street, N.W. (1980)

The entire east side of 7th Street between F and G Streets stands devoid of buildings, cleared for the construction of the Gallery Place station and other portions of Washington's new Metro subway system, parts of which were opened in 1976. The block had already suffered heavily in the riots of 1968. The station entrance may be seen at the right, marked with an "M." A huge complex, including a shopping center, hotel, and business offices, has been planned to fill the whole square block to 6th Street.

F Street, Looking West from 7th Street, N.W. (ca. 1895)

When Masonic Hall (just left of the Patent Office) was completed in 1870 on the site of the Model Hotel, F Street was still largely residential. Commercial development followed rapidly. The LeDroit Building (left) was built in 1875, the massive Washington Loan and Trust Building (left of center) in 1891. One of the city's original drinking-water sources, once an open spring, lies below 9th and F Streets.

F Street, Looking West from 7th Street, N.W. (1980)

In the early 1970s, this stretch of F Street became a park plaza, closed to vehicular traffic. The LeDroit Building, now in use as a center for artist's studios, is one of the best-preserved of Washington's remaining commercial buildings of its period. Most of the other nineteenth-century buildings in the earlier photograph have also survived. The Patent Office building had its front altered in 1936 to permit the widening of F Street. One of the capital's great early buildings, this venerable Greek Revival structure was rescued from the wrecker's ball in 1962; it now is home of the National Portrait Gallery, administered by the Smithsonian Institution.

9th Street and Louisiana Avenue, N.W. (ca. 1910)

The Bijou Theatre was the latest of a series of theaters to occupy the center building, dating from 1853 and rebuilt in 1873 after a fire. This neighborhood, south of the old Post Office, whose tower is visible over the roof of the theater, included a variety of commercial establishments. One such was James F. Oyster's wholesale outlet for butter, cheese, and eggs (right).

9th Street and Constitution Avenue, N.W. (1980)

All the buildings in the older photograph came down in the 1920s for the Federal Triangle project, which totally altered the character of the neighborhood. The Justice Department Building, seen here, was completed in 1935.

9th Street and Louisiana Avenue, N.W.,
Looking Southwest (ca. 1900)

Across the street from the scene in the previous sequence, this row of wholesale and retail meat markets bordered on Center Market (just outside of the camera's range, to the left). In the distance at the right is a smokestack of the Potomac Electric Power Company station. This part of the street then called Louisiana Avenue (another street has since been given this name) no longer exists.

9th Street and Constitution Avenue, N.W.,
Looking Southwest (1980)

Not only has the old Louisiana Avenue vanished, but all of the buildings in the previous photograph (unless the Washington Monument is counted) were demolished for the Federal Triangle project. On nearby Constitution Avenue, the National Museum of Natural History (1911) now stands not far from the old meat markets. It is one of the many magnificent museums and government buildings that now line this major boulevard of the nation's capital.

Looking Northeast from the Washington Monument (ca. 1908)

Just above the Post Office in this panoramic view is the old Post Office it replaced. Behind the tower of the newer facility may be seen the Patent Office. At the left is the Raleigh Hotel as it appeared between 1898 and 1911 and to its right is the new Star Building. Busy Center Market surrounded by a clutter of horse-drawn wagons is visible at the right. Except for the Post Office, all of the buildings between Pennsylvania Avenue and the Mall were soon to vanish.

Looking Northeast from the Washington Monument (1980)

The new Post Office, having become the old Post Office, stands nestled among its successor and other government buildings of a more recent period. The Federal Triangle project, commenced in 1928, was responsible for much of the dramatic growth seen in this photograph. Lining the north side of Constitution Avenue are the Commerce Department Building (lower left), the Post Office Building, the Internal Revenue Service Building, the Justice Department Building, the National Archives Building, and the Federal Trade Commission Building. On the south side of Constitution Avenue (lower right) is the much newer Museum of American History (1964; through 1980 called the Museum of History and Technology), a branch of the Smithsonian.

Looking South from the Washington Monument (ca. 1917)

East Potomac Park (center), then the site of a popular bathing beach bordering the Tidal Basin (right), was created by dredging and landfill operations a few years before this photograph was made. Part of the old Bureau of Printing and Engraving (1879) may be seen at the lower left. The Bureau's newer, Classic Revival building (1914) stands above it, and at the bottom of this view is a cluster of World War I temporary structures.

Looking South from the Washington Monument (1980)

The most notable addition to this scene is the Jefferson Memorial (right), dedicated in 1943. Above it, on landfill across the Potomac, are the runways of Washington National Airport (1935). The last of the wartime structures was removed in the 1950s. Modern express highways and new bridges now cross the region. To the right of center in this view an Amtrak passenger train is about to cross the Potomac. Above it is a complex of buildings belonging to the National Park Service.

Looking Southeast from the Washington Monument (1938)

At the center of this June 1938 photograph is the sprawling South Building of the U.S. Department of Agriculture, completed in 1936. The Administration Building (1931), flanked by its earlier-completed wings (1908), is attached to the South Building by enclosed walkways arching over Independence Avenue. Southwest Washington still had extensive residential areas at this time.

Looking Southeast from the Washington Monument (1980)

Most of old residential Southwest Washington has given way to complexes of apartments and government buildings. Above the Department of Agriculture's South Building is L'Enfant Plaza, including a hotel and three office buildings; to the left of that complex is the concave-sided building of the Department of Housing and Urban Development (1968). The unusual building supported on concrete pillars (left of center) is the James Forrestal Building (1970).

Looking West from Smithsonian Tower (ca. 1870)

The cornerstone of the Washington Monument was laid on July 4, 1848, and work proceeded until 1854. For 26 years the monument remained as this photograph depicts it (it was finally completed in 1884). Notice that, at this time, wetlands, seen behind the monument, reached almost to its base. Landfill operations that came to effect a radical change in the capital's geography were about to commence. The old Department of Agriculture Building stands at the left.

Looking West from Smithsonian Tower (1980)

The environs of the Washington Monument bear little resemblance to what they were 110 years earlier. Behind the Monument is the Lincoln Memorial (1922) with its Reflecting Pool. At the extreme left is the new Department of Agriculture Building (1908, 1931), replacing the old one, which was finally demolished in 1936. The Mall grounds have been relandscaped in a rectilinear pattern, following the plans of the McMillan Commission. Behind the Monument to the right is Constitution Gardens, and in the background rise the office towers of Rosslyn, Virginia. Since 1959, the base of the Washington Monument has been decorated by a circle of American flags.

Looking West from the Washington Monument (ca. 1895)

At the time of this photograph Potomac Flats, the present site of the Lincoln Memorial, was being dredged, filled, and reshaped (in a project that lasted from 1885 to 1920). Various proposals for use of the land were debated for many years until Potomac Park was created by an act of Congress on June 3, 1897. Just barely visible on a hilltop across the Potomac is the Custis-Lee Mansion (1802–4; now the Robert E. Lee Memorial), considered the first true Greek Revival structure in the Washington area.

Looking West from the Washington Monument (1980)

This section of Potomac Park, framed by Independence Avenue (left) and Constitution Avenue (right), has undergone considerable development since 1897. The small, domed structure toward the left is the District of Columbia World War I Memorial Pavilion. At the right, bordering the irregular pool, is Constitution Gardens, created for the Bicentennial (1976) after the temporary wartime Munitions and Navy buildings (erected 1917) were demolished (the last temporary structure was torn down in 1971). The Lincoln Memorial and its Reflecting Pool dominate the park. The classic marble structure, dedicated in 1922, was designed by Henry Bacon; the seated figure of Lincoln is by Daniel Chester French; and murals and ornamentation on the bronze ceiling beams are by Jules Guerin. Behind the Memorial, the Arlington Memorial Bridge (1926) crosses the river to the Arlington National Cemetery. At the right the more recent Theodore Roosevelt Memorial Bridge (1960) leads to the clustered towers of Rosslyn. Part of the John F. Kennedy Center for the Performing Arts (1971) appears on the Washington bank of the Potomac at the extreme right.

121

Looking Northwest from the Washington Monument (ca. 1894)

In 1894 the neighborhood called Foggy Bottom presented a relatively desolate appearance to spectators viewing it from the Washington Monument. Landfill operations using mule-drawn wagons may be seen in progress in the vicinity of the Washington Canal lock keeper's house (1832; bottom, right of center). Above the lock house and slightly to the right is the Van Ness Mansion (1813–17), the work of Benjamin H. Latrobe. This distinguished residence was soon demolished. The Christian Heurich Brewery (1894) stands on the Potomac at the left.

Looking Northwest from the Washington Monument (ca. 1914)

By 1914, landfill and landscaping operations give the whole area a tidier appearance. Near the site of the Van Ness Mansion is the elegant new Pan American Union Building (1908). To its right stands the also-recent headquarters of the Daughters of the American Revolution (1907).

Looking Northwest from the Washington Monument (ca. 1922)

During World War I the appearance of the area again changed radically as a result of the erection of temporary government buildings. Prominent in this ca. 1922 photograph are the temporary Munitions and Navy buildings. Behind them to the left is the brand-new Lincoln Memorial.

Looking Northwest from the Washington Monument (1980)

The area to the north is now covered with a multitude of buildings devoted to cultural, residential, governmental, diplomatic, and other purposes. On the horizon at the right stands the National Cathedral, begun in 1907 and still under construction.

B Street, West of 17th Street, N.W.,
Looking Southeast (1895)

This remarkably sharp photograph shows work in progress to improve B Street (later to become Constitution Avenue) in the shadow of the eleven-year-old Washington Monument. To the right of the Monument is the old building of the Bureau of Printing and Engraving (1879). The stone structure at the left is the lock keeper's house of the old Washington Canal. In the distance (far left) can be discerned the Gothic towers of the Smithsonian Institution.

Constitution Avenue, West of 17th Street, N.W.,
Looking Southeast (1980)

Though Constitution Avenue, here lined with modern motor vehicles, has been vastly improved, many of the structures visible in the 1895 photograph remain: the Smithsonian, the Bureau of Printing and Engraving (both obscured in this photograph), the Washington Monument, of course, and even the old lock keeper's house.

Virginia Avenue and G Street, N.W., Looking Northwest (1963)

This portion of Foggy Bottom is on the site of a very small community by the name of Funk's Town, dating back before the founding of the capital. Smokestacks of various local utility companies rise in the background. The small, blank-sided building up the avenue is a new Howard Johnson's Motor Lodge (1963). To its right is the Potomac Plaza Apartments (1957) and at the extreme right a corner of a building owned by the American Association of University Women (1959).

Virginia Avenue and G Street, N.W., Looking Northwest (1983)

This view has changed little in twenty years, except for the dramatic appearance of the Watergate complex (left). Opened in 1965 and completed in 1970, Watergate consists of three apartment buildings, two office buildings, a luxury hotel, and a shopping arcade with restaurants.

M Street Bridge over Rock Creek, Looking North (1870)

A horsecar crosses Rock Creek on its way to Southeast Washington. In colonial times the stream was forded at this point. George Washington crossed on unsecured logs in order to place the cornerstone of the Capitol. A number of bridges were constructed on the site over the years. In 1870, the light-gauge iron-truss bridge seen in this view was opened. Rock Creek at that time was navigable as far as P Street.

M Street Bridge over Rock Creek, Looking North (1980)

The 1870 bridge was replaced in 1928 by the present three-spanned concrete-and-steel-girder bridge. The Rock Creek and Potomac Parkway, a major north-south artery, now runs under the bridge alongside Rock Creek. The roadway was widened and the stream rechanneled in the 1970s.

Rock Creek Park, South Ford (1922)

Rock Creek meanders through its valley, over rough and smooth terrain. An automobile crosses the stream where bison, elk, bears, and wolves once roamed. A wagon road fording it at a shallow spot was once a popular shortcut from Northwest Washington to downtown. Whereas other cities have had to create artificially landscaped parks, Washington was always fortunate to have this naturally wooded, picturesque retreat close to its center.

Rock Creek Park, Overlooking South Ford (1980)

Visible among the trees (above and slightly left of center) is the now-closed ramp of old South Ford. Rock Creek Park is now under the jurisdiction of the National Park Service.

Wisconsin Avenue at O Street, N.W., Looking North (1893)

A horse-drawn streetcar, about to cross the main street of the Georgetown section, is on its way to downtown Washington. Off on the side streets stood the old houses that, now restored, continue to be prized as residences. Georgetown was a thriving community before Washington was even an idea. It enjoyed its own charter and self-government until 1871, when Congress brought it under the jurisdiction of D.C. government.

Wisconsin Avenue at O Street, N.W., Looking North (1983)

Horsecars gave way to electric streetcars near the turn of the century. The last of those passed this corner in 1958, when they were replaced by buses like the one emerging from O Street here. The architecture on Georgetown's main street has changed relatively little in the course of nearly a century.

Looking Across the Potomac to 36th Street, N.W. (ca. 1864)

The Aqueduct Bridge, designed by Major William Turnbull and constructed from 1833 to 1843, is seen here with its original queen-post truss and wooden superstructure. It was a bridge not for land vehicles but for boats on the C & O Canal, enabling them to carry their cargo across the Potomac to Virginia. During the Civil War a roadway replaced the boat channel. Afterward the boat channel was restored and a road built over it. The bridge was closed in 1923 when the Francis Scott Key Bridge, about a hundred feet to the east, was opened. Key himself had once lived in a house near the Georgetown entrance to the old bridge. The Key house, much deteriorated, was razed for highway construction in 1935.

Looking Across the Potomac to 36th Street, N.W. (1980)

The graceful arches of the Key Bridge span the Potomac just east of where an old pier of the Aqueduct Bridge is still visible. Many old Georgetown houses, some dating back to the 1770s, remain, now occupied as private residences and maintained as historic treasures.

Looking North from Virginia to Georgetown (1864)

Georgetown University (founded in 1789 by John Carroll, the first Archbishop of Baltimore) is the oldest Catholic college in the United States. The old North building (far right) was erected in 1795. From its porch George Washington addressed a gathering of students in 1797. At the riverside (far left) is Henry Foxhall's Foundry, where cannon were made for the war of 1812. An arched pipe of the Meigs Aqueduct (right of center) can be seen passing over a creek. The aqueduct brought water from Maryland to the District of Columbia.

Looking North from Virginia to Georgetown (1980)

The soaring Gothic spire of the University's gray granite Healy Building (1877) may be seen at the right. Federal, Classic Revival, Victorian, and twentieth-century "International" style buildings stand side by side on the rolling campus. Above the Potomac the wall of the C & O Canal and Canal Road may still be seen, though the canal was closed to commercial traffic in 1923.

Looking South from Georgetown to Virginia (1897)

Virginia, still mostly rural, may be viewed across the Potomac in this wintry scene. The part of the state glimpsed here was included in the original boundaries of the District of Columbia. In 1846, Congress restored it to the Commonwealth of Virginia. The roadway across the Aqueduct Bridge (center) conceals the boat trough, constructed over the bridge's original piers, that served as a connection to the old C & O Canal. On the near bank, to the left of the bridge, is an old canal toll house. At the extreme left is the recently constructed Capital Traction Company Union Station (1895–97), where District streetcars were turned and stored.

Looking South From Georgetown to Virginia (1983)

An original pier of the Aqueduct Bridge is visible in the center of this view. The Francis Scott Key Bridge replaced the Aqueduct Bridge in 1923 and may be seen here some yards downstream from the site of the older span. Underneath, on the Georgetown side, is an entrance to the Whitehurst Freeway, connecting Georgetown with downtown Washington. On the Virginia side, the George Washington Memorial Parkway (to accommodate which the bridge was lengthened in 1939) connects the Pentagon, Alexandria, and other areas to the south with northern suburbs. Another story was added to the Capital Traction Company station after the turn of the century. Across the Potomac, the modern office towers of Rosslyn—a spillover from downtown Washington, where office space is scarce—stand in sharp contrast to the rolling meadows of the earlier view.

Looking North to Georgetown from Virginia (1910)

This interesting view from the Virginia entrance to the Aqueduct Bridge shows the streetcar station bustling with activity. In this area, streetcars used trolley poles and overhead wires, in contrast to those in downtown Washington, which drew their power from an electrified third rail in a trough between the tracks. The Capital Traction Company Union Station (left of center) can be seen across the river in Georgetown.

Looking North to Georgetown from Virginia (1981)

The crew of rowers in the middle of the Potomac is a reminder that the original piers of the old Aqueduct Bridge were blasted out to a depth of twelve feet by U.S. Army engineers in 1962 (though the bridge had been closed since 1923), clearing the river for several lanes of rowing competition and boating. The remaining pier (left) shows clearly the trough once used by C & O Canal boats. No streetcars remain in Washington, and the Capital Traction Company Union Station has been converted to an office building. At the right, modern motor vehicles cross the Key Bridge.

Chesapeake & Ohio Canal, Above the Aqueduct Bridge,
Georgetown (1910)

Barges are lined up on the old Chesapeake & Ohio Canal, waiting for wharf space in Georgetown. This 1910 view of canal traffic belies the commonly held notion that this waterway was virtually abandoned after the first twenty years of its operation. The Baltimore & Ohio Railroad competed with the canal almost from the beginning, yet it had less of an effect on canal traffic than has been thought. The 182-mile-long canal, most of which parallels the Potomac, raised or lowered boats a total of 605 feet by means of 74 locks. The first major portion of the canal, beginning at Georgetown, then a major trading center, was opened in 1831. The tower in the background is that of the Commercial Traction Company Union Station.

Chesapeake & Ohio Canal, Above the Site of the Aqueduct Bridge, Georgetown (1980)

The old canal still exists, though it was closed to commercial traffic in 1923. The section above the site of the Aqueduct Bridge, as seen here, is now popular with hikers, strollers, and joggers. The Commercial Traction Company's tower remains, though for the most part the calm of nature has superseded the bustle of commerce.

Tidal Basin Beach, at the Future Site
of the Jefferson Memorial (1922)

A bevy of beauties frolics on the future site of the Jefferson Memorial. The Tidal Basin beach was a popular recreation area from 1916, when the Army Corps of Engineers created it as part of an extensive land-reshaping project, until 1925, when pollution led President Coolidge to close it to the public. The huge Classic Revival building of the Bureau of Printing and Engraving (1914) stands behind the women, with the Bureau's older facility (1879) to the left. The photograph was apparently taken for journalistic or publicity purposes.

Jefferson Memorial (1980)

A family of sightseers ascends the steps of the Memorial to President Thomas Jefferson, begun in 1938 and dedicated in 1943, on the site of the Tidal Basin beach. The facilities of the Bureau of Printing and Engraving remain, with new additions.